A New True Book

DINOSAUR
NATIONAL MONUMENT

By David Petersen

CHILDRENS PRESS ®

CHICAGO

View from Harpers Corner overlook
in Dinosaur National Monument

PHOTO CREDITS
American Museum of Natural History–
Neg. #2417, 6; Neg. #36246, 7
© Reinhard Brucker–2, 22, 23, 26 (inset),
32, 42, 43 (inset)
Carnegie Museum of Natural History–15,
16
Photri–19
© Branson Reynolds–8, 13, 14, 26, 34
(bottom), 44 (2 photos)
Tom Stack & Associates–© Brian Parker,
9, 36 (right); © John Cancalosi, 34 (top
left); © Wendy Shattil/Bob Rozinski, 45
SuperStock International, Inc.–© Carlton
Meyer, cover; © Gerard Fritz, 4 (2 photos),
10; © G. Martin, 20
Tony Stone Images–© Paul Damien, 43
Travel Stock–© Buddy Mays, 24, 25, 40
Unicorn Stock Photos–© John Ward, 30
UPI/Bettmann–17
Valan–© Jeff Foott, 33; © Jean Sloman, 34
(top right); © Michael J. Johnson, 36 (left)
Visuals Unlimited–© Richard Thom, 28;
© David H. Ellis, 38
Map by Tom Dunnington–21
COVER: Archaeologist at quarry wall,
Dinosaur National Monument

Project Editor: Fran Dyra
Design: Margrit Fiddle
Photo Research: Feldman & Associates, Inc.

Library of Congress Cataloging-in-Publication Data

Petersen, David.
    Dinosaur National Monument / by David Petersen.
      p.   cm.–(A New true book)
    Includes index.
    ISBN 0-516-01074-3
    1. Dinosaur National Monument (Colo. and Utah)–
Juvenile literature.   I. Title.   II. Series.
F832.D5.P48 1995   94-35655
978.8'12–dc20   CIP
                                             AC

TABLE OF CONTENTS

During the Mesozoic era, giant creatures called plesiosaurs lived in the sea, while huge flying reptiles ruled the skies (above), and dinosaurs (below) roamed the land.

AGE OF THE DINOSAURS

Imagine yourself back in time. *Way* back, all the way to the Age of the Dinosaurs. This ancient time is known as the Mesozoic era. It reached its height about 160 million years ago, during the Jurassic period.

The Jurassic period was an important time in the earth's history. At that time, many dinosaurs lived in an area that is now

Apatosaurus was a plant eater. It was one of the largest of the dinosaurs.

part of Colorado and Utah. Many of the dinosaurs were plant-eaters called *sauropods.* Among the largest of the sauropods was *apatosaurus* (also known as *brontosaurus*). Adult apatosaurs were more

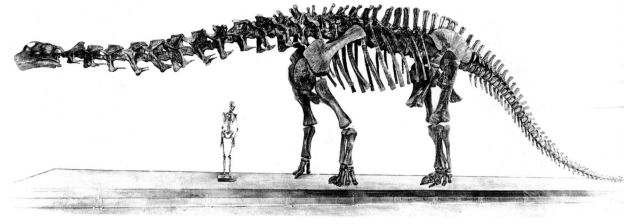

These skeletons show how a man compares in size to an *apatosaurus.*

than 70 feet long (21 meters)
and weighed up to 35 tons
(31.5 metric tons). Their tall,
giraffe-like necks allowed them
to graze on the tender tops
of high trees.

Another big plant-eating
dinosaur was *stegosaurus.*
It had two rows of big
bony fins along its back,
plus four mighty spikes at

This replica of a *stegosaurus* is on display at Dinosaur National Monument.

the end of its thick tail. Stegosaurs may have used their fins and spikes for protection against carnivorous, or flesh-eating, dinosaurs.

The king of the carnivores was *allosaurus.*

This ferocious killer was about 30 feet long (9 meters), and it was armed with three big claws on each "hand." Its gigantic mouth bristled with teeth as sharp as knives.

The huge head and teeth of *allosaurus* show that it was a fierce carnivore.

These models show triceratops being attacked by a *tyrannosaurus,* one of the largest and fiercest of the carnivores.

For millions of years, apatosaurs, stegosaurs, allosaurs, and other dinosaurs lived and died in what is now Dinosaur National Monument. When they died, many of their bones were buried in the mud of a shallow river.

BONE TO STONE

The Jurassic period ended
about 67 million years
ago. The ancient river
slowly disappeared, along
with the grasslands and
the forests. Millions of years
passed. The mud, sand,
and other river-bottom
sediments hardened into
sedimentary rock.

The buried dinosaur
bones also changed with
time. As the bones
decayed, they absorbed a

mineral called silica. Gradually, the silica hardened to stone. In this way, the dinosaur bones became fossils. They formed bone-shaped rocks.

After many more years, pressure deep in the earth began to wrinkle and fold the land that lay east of the buried bones. This geologic activity formed the Rocky Mountains.

During this upheaval, the rock layers containing the

The rocks of Dinosaur National Monument were tilted by forces within the earth.

fossilized dinosaur bones were tilted almost on end. Then the soil covering the rock was carried away by wind, rain, ice, and the rushing water of new rivers. So, once again, the rock of the ancient riverbed was exposed to the elements. The forces of erosion slowly wore away the soft sandstone of the river rock. Finally, a few of the fossilized dinosaur bones were revealed.

Dinosaur bones are visible in the rocky walls at the monument. The forces of erosion have worn away the rock to expose the fossils.

DISCOVERY

Earl Douglass was sent to Utah to search for dinosaur bones.

In 1908, the Carnegie Museum of Pittsburgh, Pennsylvania, sent Earl Douglass to Utah in search of dinosaur bones. Earl Douglass was a paleontologist–a scientist who studies fossils.

In his diary entry for August 17, 1909, Douglass wrote: "At last, in the top of the ledge I saw eight

15

Earl Douglass and his workers discovered the fossils of many kinds of dinosaurs near the Green River in Utah.

tail bones of a brontosaurus . . . It was a beautiful sight."

Over several years, Douglass and his workers dug thousands of fossilized dinosaur bones from a hillside quarry. Most of those bones are now on display at the Carnegie Museum in Pittsburgh.

A NATIONAL MONUMENT IS BORN

Within a few years of its discovery, the hillside quarry became known as one of the most important dinosaur graveyards in the world.

At the hillside quarry, the layers of sandstone were cut away to reveal the dinosaur bone fossils.

But the quarry was threatened by mining and other human activities. In 1915, to preserve this national treasure, President Woodrow Wilson granted protection to the quarry and 80 acres (32 hectares) of land surrounding it.

Excavation continued at the quarry, but the dinosaur bones were not always removed. Instead, many fossils were uncovered and left in place on the hillside. They remained exactly where

Many dinosaur fossils were uncovered but left in place at the hillside quarry.

they had lain for millions
of years.

Dinosaur National
Monument is very special.
It is one of the few places
in the world where
dinosaur fossils can be
viewed and studied in
their natural setting.

Rabbit Bush Island Park is one of the scenic
places at Dinosaur National Monument.

MORE THAN
A BONE MUSEUM

The land within Dinosaur
National Park is wild and
beautiful. In 1938, to
protect the heart of this

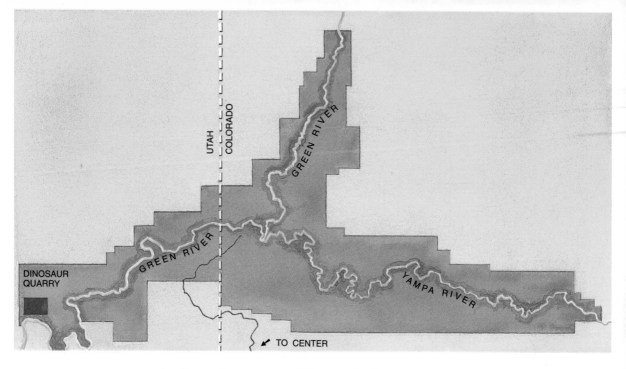

special place, President
Franklin D. Roosevelt
enlarged the park.

Today, Dinosaur National
Monument stretches east and
north into Colorado, giving
the monument the shape
of an upside-down T. The
park also includes about

21

The Green River flows through Dinosaur National Monument.

100 miles (161 kilometers) of the lovely Green and Yampa rivers.

Roads enter Dinosaur in several places. A few of them are paved, but most are rugged dirt trails.

Cub Creek Drive is a dirt road that
winds through the wilderness of Dinosaur.

Therefore, automobile traffic
is limited.

Walking is a far more
enjoyable way to see
Dinosaur. Hiking trails lead
to hidden canyons,
overlooks, waterfalls, and

other exciting places away from the roads.

But most of the park has neither roads nor hiking trails, making Dinosaur a true wilderness.

This hiker explores a very narrow canyon in Dinosaur.

Dinosaur skeleton on display at the Headquarters Visitor Center

EXPLORING DINOSAUR NATIONAL MONUMENT

Your first stop at Dinosaur should be the Headquarters Visitor Center near the tiny town of Dinosaur, Colorado. There you will see

exhibits and a slide show. Friendly park rangers will help you make the most of your stay at this fascinating national monument.

From the center, the 62-mile (100-kilometer) Harpers Corner scenic drive winds through fantastic desert and steep canyons.

Along the way, stop at Canyon, Island Park, Iron Springs Bench, and Echo Park overlooks. You'll enjoy their dazzling views of the

Opposite page: The Green River flowing through Whirlpool Canyon and (inset) a view from Echo Park overlook

The Yampa and Green River canyons can be seen from the Harpers Corner nature trail.

monument's wilderness interior.

At road's end, stretch your legs and hike the 2-mile (3.2-kilometer) Harpers Corner nature trail. Views from this trail include Echo Park, where the Yampa River joins the Green, as well as Whirlpool and Yampa canyons.

Of special interest for young people is Red Rock Nature Trail. On this trail, the signs explaining nature were not written by adults. They were written by young people, especially for young people.

At nightfall, you can pitch your tent or park your travel trailer in Dinosaur. There are two campgrounds near the dinosaur quarry.

This campground is at the base of Split Mountain,
which rises near the Green River in Dinosaur.

Many campsites in these campgrounds lie along the Green River, shaded by giant cottonwood trees. And both of these big campgrounds have restrooms and running water.

And if you prefer a more daring camping experience, you can always rough it at Dinosaur. Pitch your tent at one of the park's remote primitive campgrounds.

This rock carving of a lizard was made by ancient people who camped in the Dinosaur area.

ANCIENT VISITORS

Modern tourists were not the first people to camp in this area. For thousands of years, Native American people hunted and camped in what is now Dinosaur Monument.

The ancient Indians are long gone, but signs of their presence remain. You

Ancient Native American art at Dinosaur shows people and animals.

can see their rock paintings, called pictographs, and rock carvings, called petroglyphs, throughout Dinosaur.

The wilderness of Dinosaur is home to many species of animals, including bighorn sheep (top left), cougars (top right), and collared lizards.

WILDLIFE AT DINOSAUR

If you enjoy watching wildlife, you'll love Dinosaur National Monument. Many wild creatures live within the protection of the monument. You'll see lizards, snakes, deer, rabbits, squirrels, elk, mountain lions, and a variety of birds. Dinosaur is also home to the rare and shy desert bighorn sheep.

The river otter (left) and the endangered Colorado squawfish are two rare animals that can be seen at Dinosaur.

Along the rivers, you may spot ducks, geese, and the bark-and-mud dams and lodges of beavers. If you're very lucky, you might even catch a glimpse of a rare river otter.

And down in the murky depths of the Green and Yampa rivers swim four of the rarest fish in America. They are the Colorado squawfish, the roundtail chub, the humpback chub, and the razorback sucker. These are not "pretty" fish, but they are important members of the native ecology.

Another endangered species protected at Dinosaur is the beautiful peregrine falcon. The

The beautiful peregrine falcon hunts its prey from high above the canyons and deserts of Dinosaur.

peregrine hunts other birds, and can dive at nearly 200 miles (322 kilometers) per hour to catch its prey in flight.

Dinosaur is a sanctuary for several other rare wild animals and plants. Outside the park, their survival is threatened by human activities.

RUN A RIVER!

In wet years, the Green and Yampa rivers boom with floodwaters in spring and early summer. Melting snow in distant mountains causes these waters to rise.

As the swollen rivers speed through narrow canyons, they roar and crash over and around rocks, forming rapids.

If you like excitement, take a trip through Dinosaur's rapids. Several

Rafters running the Green River

river outfitters provide
sturdy rafts and
experienced river guides.
  "Running" a river through
Dinosaur is one of the
most thrilling adventures
anyone could ever have!

DINOSAUR QUARRY

Of course, the dinosaur quarry draws most visitors to this remote western national monument.

Back in 1957, a tall, three-sided building was erected over the hillside quarry to protect the fossils from erosion and theft. The quarry hill itself provides the building's fourth wall.

The quarry building is built against a wall of exposed dinosaur fossils.

The quarry building also serves as a museum and visitors' center. There you can watch paleontologists at work. Each year, thousands of people from all over the world come to see the famous wall of dinosaur bones.

When the wall of fossils was first found, scientists removed many of the bones and sent them to the Carnegie Museum in Pittsburgh. Now the wall is protected by the Visitor Center building (inset).

Above: Turtle Rock seen from Cub Creek Drive
Below: Split Mountain seen from Harpers Corner

An adult
peregrine
falcon with
its chicks
in their
cliffside nest

Dinosaur bones, deserts, canyons, rivers, hiking, rafting, camping, prehistoric Indian art, and wildlife all wait for *you* at Dinosaur National Monument in Utah and Colorado. A place where the West is still wild!

45

WORDS YOU SHOULD KNOW

endangered species (en • DAIN • jerd SPEE • seez)–plants and animals in great danger of disappearing

erosion (ih • ROH • zhun)–the wearing away of the earth's surface by wind, water, ice, and other natural forces

fossil (FAW • sil)–the hardened remains of an animal or plant that lived long ago

Jurassic period (joo • RASS • ik)–a time in the earth's history that lasted from 205 million to 138 million years ago

paleontologist (pail • ee • en • TAH • luh • jist)–a scientist who studies the fossil remains of life from past periods of the earth's history

quarry (KWAW • ree)–a place where fossils or minerals are dug, or excavated, from the ground

rapids (RAP • ids)–dangerous places in rivers where the water runs very fast over rocks or other obstructions

sauropods (SOR • oh • podz)–a group of plant-eating dinosaurs that had long necks and tails and small heads

sediments (SED • ih • ments)–small particles, such as mud and sand, deposited on the bottom of a body of water

sedimentary rock (sed • ih • MEN • tree ROK)–soft rock that forms when a body of water dries up and its sediments harden into stone. Sandstone, limestone, and shale are three kinds of sedimentary rock.

INDEX

About the Author

David Petersen has written more than two dozen books of natural history for children and adults. When not writing or teaching college, he spends his time exploring the West from his cabin in the San Juan Mountains of southwest Colorado.